P9-CQY-238

ENTHUSIA SMALL

[En-thu-si-asm All]

Dear Reader,

It's not every day that a book idea steps up and introduces itself. But such was the case with *Dig It!* when a gentleman approached us at a Postmark Naperville book signing and handed us his business card.

"So what's a privy digger?" we asked. After listening to his stories and seeing his artifacts, we looked at each other and said, "There's a book in this." And here it is.

Before the days of trash pick-up and recycling, broken, bruised and unwanted items were daily discards down the privy. The quantity and variety of recovered artifacts is stunning. The fascination with this hobby is the peephole it provides into other days and other ways of life.

Join us as we spotlight privy artifacts of the Midwest. And remember, every single artifact was actually dug from an abandoned outhouse hole.

Imagine that.

MKM & SRW

Dig It!

Privy Artifacts A-Z

**By Sharon Ridgeway Weber
and Marcia Koffron Mackenbrock**

Published by Enthusia Small
http://www.enthusiasmall.com

Graphic Design by Lisa D. Klingbeil
West Branch Studio, Naperville, IL
http://www.westbranchstudio.com

To Tom and Nancy Majewski who took us into an
underground world where few have dared to dig and
who added a whole new depth to our vocabularies.

Acknowledgments

Heartfelt thanks to the following people who stepped forward when we needed them and
who shared our vision for this unique project:

John Wilson - who selflessly shared his time, knowledge and artifacts.

Lisa Klingbeil - who proved it really is possible to turn a sow's ear into a silk purse.

Erika Ridgeway - who created the sassy "potty mouth" faces.

Karen and Andy Knight - who permitted an actual dig on their property.

Becky Anderson Wilkins - who encouraged and promoted our endeavor.

Mary Garry - who is always on the lookout for "fabulous" stuff.

Mike Bowers - who created the privy digger business card logo.

John A. Klepacki, CDT - who provided dental research relating to the 1800s.

John Holecsek - who assisted with German translation.

Property owners - who allowed their artifacts to be photographed.

ISBN 0-9754040-1-6
Copyright © 2006 by Enthusia Small
ISBN 978-0-9754040-1-0

Table of Contents

All About Tom
= Privy Digger

Above: S & P twins. Not privy dug.

Tom Majewski

privy (noun)

A small toilet shelter outside of a house. From the Latin word for

PRIVY DIGGER
TOM MAJEWSKI

It all began with bottles . . .

I was introduced to digging over thirty years ago, yet I remember it like it was yesterday. While cleaning the basement of a shop where I was working, I came across buckets of dirty old bottles. Out they went. I soon learned those "dirty old bottles" were over 100 years old and not intended for the trash. To hammer the lesson home, I was "invited" to spend Saturday digging with my boss at the site of a city dump dating to the 1800s.

The first three feet produced nothing but sweat and I thought this was the ultimate punishment. Another two feet and I hit a bottle. As I picked it up, a feeling came over me that I was holding something that had not seen the light of day for over 100 years. I was hooked.

For the next fifteen years my digging was primarily in old city dumps. Researching the history of my finds became my passion. But what I really wanted was to connect items to the families who used them, and I couldn't do that with things found in a city dump. Then I read about people out east who dug privies on private home sites, and the seed was planted. The local history could be fantastic!

Left: A surprise 50th birthday gift from Tom's sister, Diane.

Below: Corroded metal remains of a double-barreled shotgun. Another surprising find.

A GOOD DIG IS BETTER THAN A HOLE IN ONE!

It's always more fun, and safer, to share this hobby with a friend. I have been blessed to share my privy digs with my best friend, John Wilson. Together we've had some unique experiences. On one dig, after every shovelful of dirt, the homeowner's pet chicken insisted on jumping into the hole to eat the grubs and worms. Another dig produced an audience of seventeen people and three dogs all leaning over the hole. A close call came when the privy we thought we were digging turned out to be a capped well with a long way down and no way out. One of our deepest and best digs was under a garage. When the homeowner said we should go ahead and dig there, we were puzzled until he rolled back a piece of carpeting exposing a dirt floor. Sure enough, we found a privy dating to 1865.

While I've met new people and made new friends, I couldn't have pursued my unique hobby without the support of my family, especially my wife. She is the one who puts up with dirty boots, dirty clothes, dirty car seats, dirty buckets, late nights and early mornings. And she does it with a smile. She often brings lunch and pitches in to help give programs at local historical societies. Our two older children survived their teen years in spite of being tagged as, "the kids whose father digs in old toilets." They, too, have grown to appreciate the history behind the hobby that has given me so much enjoyment.

Truth is, I would never trade my truck full of shovels and tarps for a bag full of golf clubs. Come weekends, I choose to swing a shovel, not a club.

From my yard to yours, Tom

Below: A real beauty.

Ask Tom:

What is the most surprising artifact you ever dug?

Right: The big surprise!

Tom Says:

A porcelain toilet! Privies came before indoor plumbing, so finding this seemed backward to me.

Bottoms Up = Makers' Marks

maker's mark (noun)

A mark on the bottom of porcelain or pottery identifying location made and date.

Some porcelain pieces are more intriguing when displayed "bottoms up" for that is where the often mysterious and frequently elegant Maker's Mark is found. Beautiful and beguiling, these stamps are also a bewildering code that, when broken, can identify the country, city, factory and date of a piece of china, essential information when seeking additions to or replacements for a collection. Unearthed from a privy, they speak to the lifestyle of a bygone era.

THOSE GUYS SURE LEFT THEIR MARKS!

Ask Tom:

Have you ever researched a maker's mark to see where it originated?

Tom Says:

I've tried, but the variety is so overwhelming that just when you think you've traced one, you see a variation.

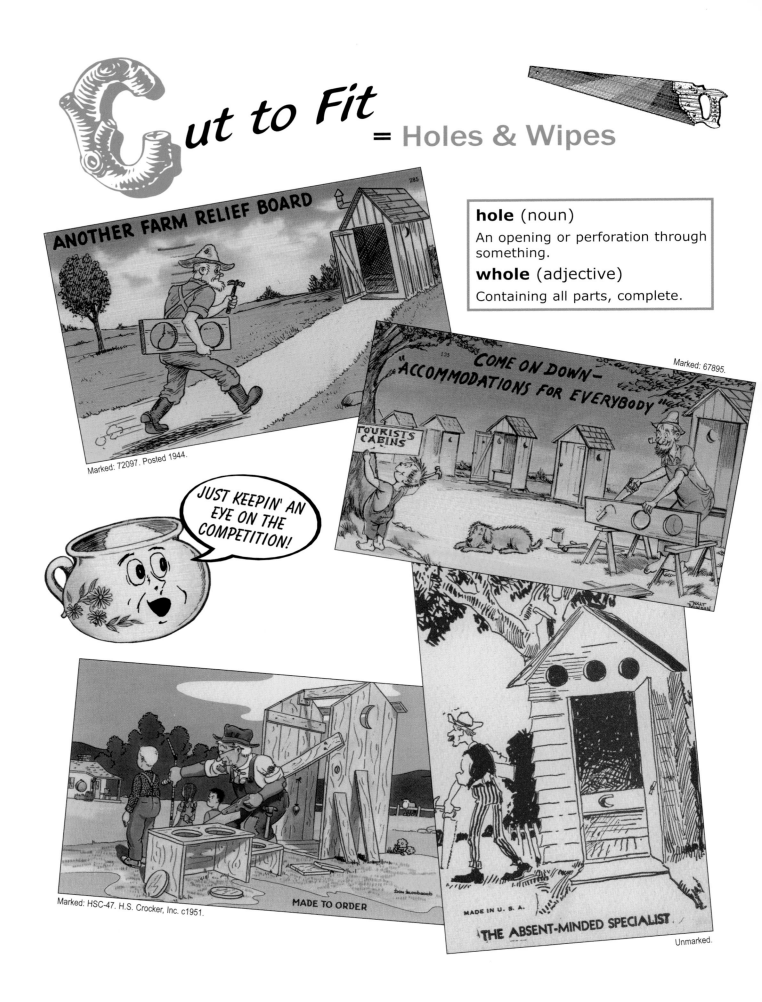

Cut to Fit = Holes & Wipes

hole (noun)
An opening or perforation through something.
whole (adjective)
Containing all parts, complete.

Before the luxury of toilet paper, privy visitors had to be resourceful. Especially popular were mail-order catalog pages. The thicker the catalog, the longer it lasted. Lacking catalogs, newspapers, corncobs and dress patterns were called into service.

Privies often sported a range of hole sizes tailor-made to fit the family. Large for adults, small for children. The holes and familiar crescent moon above the door had to be cut with a hand saw, a tricky proposition.

Marked: Metrocraft #C500.

YOU'RE SURE MISSED AT THE OLD STAND!

WHY DON'T YOU PAY US A VISIT?

Greetings from the "WHOLE" Family!

Marked: D-41194-B, U.S.A.

HI MATHILDA.......
WRITE FER ONE OF THEM NEW CATALOGS PRONTO!

Marked: Tichnor Bros., Inc. Posted 1951.

Ask Tom:

Have you ever probed a site without success?

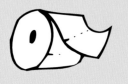

Right: Typical salt and pepper collectible pair. Not privy dug.

Tom Says:

Yes, over the years a driveway, garage or sidewalk could have been built that now covers the privy site.

Down to Earth = Excavation

excavation (noun)
To uncover or expose by digging; unearth.

HISTORICAL EXCAVATIONS DONE WITH CARE

One look at Tom's Truckload and it's obvious that privy excavation is hard work. It takes passion, patience and perseverance, but the results can be historically rewarding.

To see a dig through Tom's eyes, match these correctly and you'll know we're following him down the _____ _____. (answer found below)

1. Do the holes smell?

2. How do you feel after a dig?

3. What is your digging fee?

4. Do you find water in the holes?

5. When do you stop a dig for safety?

6. Does anything tip you off to possible sites?

7. What artifacts do you like to keep?

8. Do you ever find multiple holes in a yard?

9. What do you do with unwanted finds?

L. Would you believe a dozen?

O. Bottles are my favorites.

H. A lilac bush or a dip in the ground.

E. Homeowner's call - keep or rebury.

R. Exhilarated and exhausted.

I. Not a dime.

Y. Cracked sidewalls send us to the top.

P. Just good and earthy.

V. Not a drop.

Answers: 1. p, 2. r, 3. i, 4. v, 5. y, 6. h, 7. o, 8. l, 9. e.

Tom's Truckload:

Digging partner
Old area maps
Work gloves
Water jugs
Bug spray
Hardhat
Towel
Rope
Cap
Spade
Sod lifter
Shovels –
- Long handle
- D handle
- Small GI

Pitchfork
Handsaw
Small rake
Hand axe
Root cutters
Sledge hammer
5 gal. buckets
Plastic drop cloths
Custom length probes
Large knives
Quartz light/stand
Drop cord light
Flashlight
First aid kit
Digging boots

Ask Tom:

What is often the hardest part of the whole process?

ONE MAN'S TRASH IS ANOTHER MAN'S HOBBY!

Tom Says:

Getting permission to dig from a home owner you don't know is the most difficult.

Below: A footnote.

veryday Needs = Kitchen Collectibles

earthenware (noun)
The coarser set of containers and tableware made of baked clay.

Then as now, the one thing a kitchen could not be without was a mix of bowls. Produced in great numbers, design and band color were determined at the whim of the potter and were never twice the same. Yellowware with a raised design was considered a step above its banded brothers.

Equally vital to the cook were fruit jars in sizes varying from half pint to half gallon. Used to preserve any number of foods, fruit jars are the most common kitchen find on privy digs. Sometimes found with contents still inside, they were most likely disposed of due to broken seals. Illness and death were known to occur from improperly sealed fruit jars. Highly collectible today, bowls and jars were a dime a dozen in the 1800s.

Above: Tapered pepper sauce bottle and wide-mouth pickle jar.

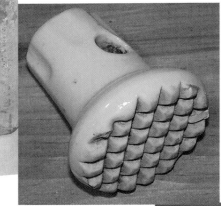

Left: Meat tenderizer minus wooden handle.

Left: Small jar "Patented April 13th 1858." Large lipped jar would have glass lid insert sealed with wax.

Right: Enamel bowl, ladle and broom pattern trivet.

BOWLS, BOWLS, BOWLS, BOWLS, Z-Z-Z-Z-Z-Z.

Above left: Yellowware bowls with raised design.

Below: Spongeware appeared on kitchen shelves later than banded bowls.

Ask Tom:

You often find ash when you dig. Where would that come from?

GRAND MEDAL OF MERIT VIENNA

JAMES KEILLER & SONS
DUNDEE
MARMALADE
PRIZE MEDAL FOR MARMALADE
LONDON, 1862
GREAT BRITAIN.

Tom Says:

Burning wood in cook stoves and fireplaces created mounds of ash that would be thrown down the privy.

*F*eel Better Fast
= Apothecaries

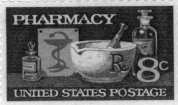

Right: Illinois bottles from:
W.C. Budlong, Aurora;
J.E. Molone, LaSalle;
John C. Neltnor, West Chicago;
Lutz & Briggs, Ottawa;
Daniels Bros., Naperville;
L.J. Patghim, Batavia;
I.N. Benton, St. Charles;
Avenue Pharmacy, Oak Park;
Bush & Simonson, Downers Grove.

Left: Embossed bottles from Naperville and Aurora, IL druggists: Holmes Bros., Aurora; D.W. Hurd Chekered Store, Aurora; M.B. Powell & Co., Naperville; Daniels Bros., Naperville; W.W. Wickell & Co. (currently Oswald's Pharmacy), Naperville; Walter F. Vogt, Naperville; Downing & Mann, Aurora; Staudt & Newmann, Aurora.

JUST HOLD YOUR NOSE AND SWALLOW.

apothecary (noun)
One who makes, sells and formerly prescribed drugs and medical preparations.

Above: Not all bottles were clear glass as shown by these striking Illinois examples: Edwin Springer & Co., Elgin; J.N. Staudt, Aurora.

Whether you were feeling under the weather, not quite up to snuff, or fighting a case of the vapors, a trip to the local druggist, "pharmaceutist" or apothecary could soon have you resting easily. Mixed on site and packaged in hand blown, paper thin glass bottles called "puffs" by collectors, these tonics were meant for one time use only and became frequent discards down the hole. If a mixture appeared to cure one person's malady, it was duly noted and prescribed for similar conditions. Drug licensing was unknown and morphine, opium and alcohol were common additives, thus assuring the patient would "feel better fast."

Above: *A collection of hand-blown, unmarked, Civil War vintage "puffs."*

Right: *Irregular lips and very uneven bottoms were typical.*

Above: *Dispensed by pharmacists for one-time use.*

 *Ask* **Tom:**

How did you decide to collect apothecary bottles?

Tom Says:

I thought it was interesting that embossed Chicago bottles showed druggists' names and addresses.

Ghastly Brews = Elixirs

Is your liver causing you grief? Do you have bilious complaints? Are your children suffering from pin worms? Elixirs to the rescue! The same patent medicines promising to cure these and a host of other human ills would likely be colorfully and imaginatively advertised as being equally effective on household pets and barnyard animals. Mass produced and sold in drug stores, they were often accompanied by stirring written testimonials. Disclosure of ingredients was not required and alcohol was often the soothing ingredient that, when "taken as directed," could cure your every ill.

Left: You name it, it cures it: Dr. J. Hostetter's Stomach Bitters, Soothing Syrup, Rheumatic Liniment.

Above: Unembossed and having paper labels, "slicks" are the most common bottles found. Note the large pontil scar on bottom and air bubbles in this early example.

Right: Warner's Safe Kidney & Liver Cure. Rochester, N.Y.

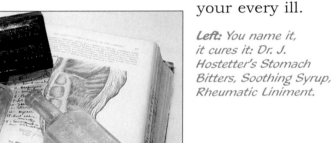

Left: An interesting claim to cure both man and beast.

Left: *Choose your poison: Ague Conqueror, Dr. Drake's German Croup Remedy, Rheumatic Liniment, Begg's Blood Purifier, A. Trast's Magnetic Ointment, Hamlin's Wizard Oil, Mrs. Winslow's Soothing Syrup or Sloan's Ointment.*

GUARANTEED TO CURE YOU OR TO KILL YOU.

Above and Left: *A collection of cure-alls: Reed's 1878 Tonic, Paine's Celery Compound, Dr. Hostetter's Stomach Bitters and Electric Bitters.*

Ask Tom:

Have you ever dug a bottle that was still sealed and full of liquid?

Tom Says:

Yes, several, but uncorked they have an awful smell.

Hold Everything = Crocks & Jugs

potsherd (noun)
A broken earthenware pottery fragment.

Restless boys, free time, loose stones and - bull's eye! A small rock blindly dropped down the hole followed by a satisfying crash. Large, thick-walled crocks, the brutes of household storage, were often purposely broken to more easily fit through seat holes.

Often dug, but seldom whole, they were used as containers for everything. To preserve foods waxed cloth was pulled taut over the opening and secured with string which was then also waxed. This kept insects and air out and odors in. They, like jugs, their liquid holding counterparts, were as common as barn cats on every homestead.

Above: Some crock designs were hand painted at the whim of the artist.

Above: Graduated crocks finished in different glazes showing hand painted gallon numbers.

Above: Everyday workhorses, crocks served as storage wherever needed.

DID SOMEONE SAY MOONSHINE?

Below: Two-tone insulated jug from Western Stoneware Co.

Above: Handle free jug for molasses or pan drippings saved from cooking to be reused. Handled jugs commonly contained whiskey, cider or various chemicals.

Below: Typical household crock, piece of unidentified blue commemorative crock and a sided mineral water pottery bottle.

Above: Wood and wire handle commonly found on large crocks. Would have deteriorated underground. Not privy dug.

Ask Tom:

Did crocks come with lids?

Tom Says:

Smaller ones often did. Larger ones might have wooden lids, but they would not be airtight.

nto the Night = Oil Lamps

THE BEST IN THE WORLD.
A COMPLETE FAMILY OIL TANK AND LAMP FILLER COMBINED.

Candlelight may have been kinder to ladies' complexions, but oil lamps banished the darkness. Quickly embraced, they were produced in a dizzying array of styles. Keeping wicks trimmed and oil reservoirs filled were daily chores. And a trip out back was better illuminated with oil than candle. But an accidental jerk of the hand, and they, too, fell prey to the privy. Although sturdy bases were more likely to survive their entombment than delicate shades, bases today are the more exciting find. When a large number of lamps were dug in a single hole, it was a sure sign the home had become "electrified."

FIRST NIGHT IN THE COUNTRY

Marked: A Colour Picture Publication. Boston, Mass.

NEXT TIME THEY SHOULD JUST WAKE ME UP!

kerosene (noun)
A thin oil used for illumination.

Below: Small (3-1/2 inch) finger lamp chimneys, 1860-1900.

Above: *Finger lamps so named for finger holds used for carrying. Would be topped with glass.*

Left: Decorative milk glass chimney shade.

Below: Oil lamp chimneys, one with an unusual oval base.

Above: Milk glass base with pressed glass oil receptacle.

Marked: Advertising card c1886.

Chimney

Oil Reservoir

Base

Right: Bullet chimney, pat. July 23, 1868.

Ask Tom:

Could fire be a hazard if a kerosene lamp fell down a hole?

Above: A trio of oil reservoirs, the center part of a three-piece lamp.

Tom Says:

Possibly. If the wick were not extinguished, the kerosene could spill and burn.

Just Blowing Smoke = Pipes

Pipe smoking has long provided an irresistible moment's ease. Privy diggers find proof of that often and in quantity but usually in pieces. In 500 digs, only a fistful of the pipes unearthed are intact. Many were early tavern giveaways that a smoker could take home or leave behind for the next patron to continue exhaling cares by snapping off a bit of stem. The distinctive tobacco aroma still haunts the recovered clay bowls a century later.

nose warmer (noun)
A short-stemmed pipe.

Above: Figural clay pipe bowls often depicted females, Presidents and people wearing turbans. An unusual example here is the skull. Most bowls were glazed.

Above: A sampling of pieces commonly found in a dig. The everyday, working man's pipe.

Marked: B.B. London & New York. Series #E2440. Printed in Germany.

HOLY SMOKES!

Above: Tobacco union label.

Right: Advertisement in 1886 Naperville, IL Business Directory.

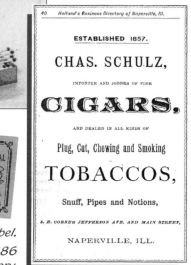

40   *Holland's Business Directory of Naperville, Ill.*

ESTABLISHED 1857.

CHAS. SCHULZ,

IMPORTER AND JOBBER OF FINE

CIGARS,

AND DEALER IN ALL KINDS OF

Plug, Cut, Chewing and Smoking

TOBACCOS,

Snuff, Pipes and Notions,

S. E. CORNER JEFFERSON AVE. AND MAIN STREET,

NAPERVILLE, ILL.

Marked: Smokers No. 190.

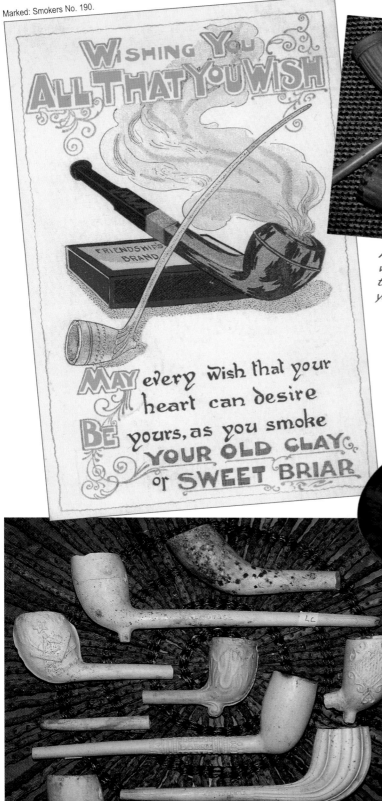

Above: Reeds are never found in digs. Made of wood, they would decompose. Readily available, they were sold in bunches. As long as you had your own reed, you could share a pipe bowl.

Above: Made in Germany, Meerschaum bowls such as this eventually put clay pipes out of business. Thought to have a finer and smoother feel than clay, they would color to darker hues and were seen as status symbols. Meerschaum is a German word meaning sea foam. Mined in Turkey and Africa, they were made of fossilized sea creatures.

Left: While most clay bowls were plain, some, like these examples, showed intricate patterns. The angled bowl at top dates to the early 1800s. The heel, or spur, seen on many of these pieces kept the pipe upright and away from surfaces that might burn.

SMOKING JACKETS.

The Newest Styles, made especially for Fine Trade.

We make prices right, and you save half or more.

See Our Clothing Dept.

July, 4, 0?
Do you remember
two years ago to-day.

Below: *To prevent breakage, pipes from abroad came packed in sawdust-filled wooden boxes like the one below.*

FRAGILE WITH CARE
CLAY TOBACCO PIPES
MANUFACTURED BY
D. McDOUGALL & Cº Lᵀᴰ
GLASGOW, Scotland.

July 23, 1901
June 24, 1906.
July, 4, 1907.

Oft in the evening twilight
We bring back memories fond,
We try to read the smoke-wreaths
And think of friendship's bond.

July, 4, 1909. My Pipe and I.

Marked: Williamson Haffner Publishers. American Series.

Ask Tom:

Would the pipes you dig still be usable today?

Right: *It is rare to find complete clay pipes. Fragile stems are usually broken and missing.*

Do not go Ashtray

Tom Says:

Probably, though it would not be as smooth a smoke. I have given some to Civil War reenactors, but I don't know if they were just props or if they actually smoked them.

Keep It Filled
= Pitchers

Without indoor plumbing for easy access to water, the pitcher was a home necessity in kitchens, bedrooms and on summer porches. An empty pitcher meant a trip to the pump.

Right: As is from the ground. Seen better days.

Below: An assembly of unadorned but shapely examples.

Above: A stately 10 1/4" tall, this decorative pitcher dates to around 1900.

PSST! FILL THOSE UP, BUT EMPTY ME.

Tom Says:

Sure. Especially in rural areas. Naperville had them until the 1950s.

Ask Tom:

Are there any privies still in use in this country?

Listen for the Pop = Sodas

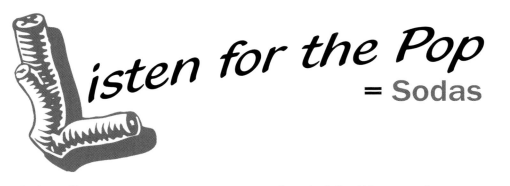

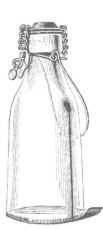

Privy diggers are no strangers to buried bottles, and almost every outhouse hole hoards them. However, privies may be the stingiest with soda bottles. Why? Because sodas were expected to be returned for refilling.

First patented in 1810, early sodas were called health water. The earliest cork stopped, "blob" style bottle was opened with an ice pick. Hutchinson style stoppers introduced the word "pop" to our vocabularies because the stopper popped when pushed into the bottle. Crown tops were introduced following the 1906 Pure Food & Drug Act to ensure empty bottles were thoroughly cleaned inside. No more corks, no more stoppers.

> **carbonate** (verb)
> To enliven a beverage with carbon dioxide gas.

The popularity of soda has never waned. In fact, in 2002 the average American drank 546 sodas or approximately 54 gallons. That's called thirst.

Trading card message:

"HIRES BEER, may be dear reader, something you have yet to try
If so, then a single package for a quarter you should buy
Make it up and drink it freely, and you never need to fear
That it will intoxicate you - 'tis the PROHIBITION BEER."

Above: "Blob" style soda bottles, 1840s-1870s. Note chipped tops where corks were dug out.

Trading card message continued:

Root Beer syrup bottles. ". . . makes 5 gallons of a most delicious sparkling temperance beverage. Strengthens and purifies the blood. Its purity and delicacy of flavor commend it to all."

Left: A basket of "Hutchinson" style bottles, 1879-1906.

Right: An easy way to identify a favorite soda was by the trademark emblem on the front. This bottle sports the "bear" brand.

Deliver prepaid to my home and charge to my account, the numbe[r] opposite the name of the article and under the size of the bottles.

Cases may be divided among the various articles to suit buyer's convenience	CASES 6 Oz. Split Size 48 Bottles $6.00	10 Oz. Club Size 48 Bottles $7.00
Billy Baxter Ginger Ale		
Billy Baxter Club Soda		
Billy Baxter Sarsaparilla		
Billy Baxter Lime Soda		
Billy Baxter Root Beer		
Billy Baxter Lemon Soda		
Temple Water Splits (50 bottles to case) $6.00		
Temple Water Pints (50 bottles to case) $7.00		
Red Raven Splits (one size only, 48 bottles to case) $6.00		
Billy Baxter's Letters (Bound & Illustrated) $1.00 per copy		

Above: A "Hutchinson" bottle named for the inventor of its stopper. When pushed into the bottle, it made a popping sound. Thus, our word soda "pop."

Above: A "crown top" bottle style and wooden crate from the Aurora Bottling Co. Box not privy dug.

Ask Tom:

Why were some soda bottles marked, "This bottle is never sold?"

Tom Says:

The bottle was meant to be returned. The consumer was buying the contents, not the bottle.

Memorable Finds
= One-of-a-Kind

find (noun)
Something found, especially something interesting.

Experienced diggers know to look to the corners of the hole when excavating a privy. Safe from the avalanche of daily waste, pieces found there are often the best preserved.

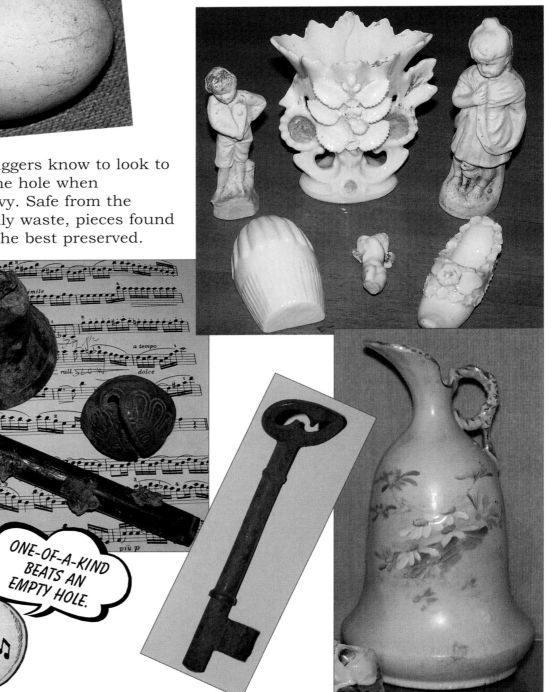

An eclectic assortment of singular discoveries from a decade of digs: a silent flute, a two inch horse tooth, an 1877 lightening rod ball and spear, and perhaps the most surprising of all, a perfectly whole egg.

Ask om:

How do people react when you first approach them to excavate?

As seen by these examples, porcelain and glass pieces weather life underground better than metal.

om Says:

Suspicious. I often show them an old Sanborn Insurance map showing their original home site and then I start explaining the process.

# No More Candles
= Light Bulbs

carbon (noun)

A filament through which current is conducted.

The invention of the light bulb in the late 1800s signaled the beginning of the end for candles and oil lamps. From humble cottages to glittering salons the light bulb was here to stay. New ones were needed and old ones were disposed of down the ever convenient privy. And there they rested.

Enter the unsuspecting privy digger, shovel in hand. One scoop, two scoops, then-BAM! Could the hole be harboring live ammunition? No, just a long dormant light bulb, its vacuum seal pierced by the shovel blade. A last hurrah from the invention that took the Victorians into a glowing future.

Below: Passé brass and copper candlesticks. Snuff the flame, flip the switch, let there be light!

Marked: Lovelights Series C.

Above: Two glass pin-type insulators used for the support and insulation of wires on outside poles.

Left: Clear when new, these used bulbs appear brown due to the burning of carbon filament.

Right: A line-up of early bulbs with porcelain or screw cap copper bases.

Marked: Made in U.S.A. #267.

Ask Tom:

How could something so delicate survive so long buried in a privy?

Tom Says:

Luck. It landed soft and nothing hard was thrown on top.

Once Behind a House
= Karen's Place

artifact (noun)
Any object made by human work.

1. Cedar Place, 1862. Fifty miles west of Chicago, IL.

2. It all begins with a probe.

3. Enter the shovel.

4. Lifting out the layers.

9. A return to the light of day.

10. A round-up of the dig's labors.

11. Refilling the hole.

12. Topping it off.

13. Replacing the turf.

14. Securing the sod with a final stomp.

UNDER THE BED SURE BEATS UNDER THE GROUND.

How do you find an abandoned privy? You listen for it. Actually, it's a fine balance between sound and touch.

In the case of Cedar Place, built in 1850, it happened after a four hour probe of rock-hard ground, working back and forth across the yard in one foot increments. Then, wait a minute. An ever-so-slight yielding of the soil and the abrasive sound of metal through crushed glass. Pure music to a trained digger's ear.

Out came shovels and tarps. Following a careful lifting of the sod, the dig began in earnest. After routine digging for the first three feet, the pace abruptly slowed. Working carefully around tree roots, the first glimmer of artifact was seen.

Knives and brushes replaced shovels to gently free long buried objects of Cedar Place history. Shards of china and glass filled a bucket and were set aside. Unbroken and recognizable pieces were cautiously carried to safety.

Once the dig was bottomed out the refilling began. It ended with no sign of disturbance left behind.

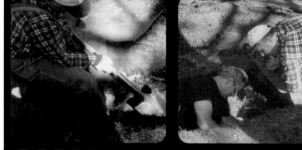
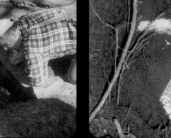
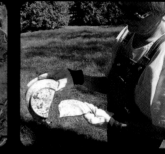

5. Slowing down for tree roots.

6. What have we here?

7. The first find.

8. Piecing together a family history.

Ask Tom:

In a house this old, what are the chances of finding multiple privies?

Karen and Andy Knight

Above: *Cedar Place, 2006.*

Tom Says:

There should be several depending on how deeply the privy was dug, how many people used it and how much trash was thrown in. A hole's life expectancy was extended if a "honey dipper" was hired to clean it.

Powder Your Nose = Vanity & Hygiene

vanity (noun)
Extreme pride in one's appearance.

Left: A man's wedding band. Gold does not deteriorate underground.

Dresser tops of the 1800s would be just as full of "lotions and potions" for beauty and hygiene as ours are today. No Victorian lady would be without perfume bottles, decorative atomizers and jars and pots of skin creams. Long hat pins held hats firmly to twisted coils of hair. Gentlemen might own a mustache cup to protect that often waxed and styled marvel of the upper lip. When tooth brushes were not sufficient to stave away decay, false teeth could be had. As for which of the sexes used the bottles of hair restorer and hair dye? That secret remains forever down the privy.

Left: A variety of items that might have been found on a lady's dressing table: brooch, cream balm jar; hair brush (minus bristles); hair barrette; buttons and an 11 inch hat pin monogrammed with an "E."

Right: Ladies' vanity bottles: two violin shaped perfumes; an aqua 7 Sutherland Sisters Hair Grower bottle; a dimpled glass atomizer and two embossed clear glass scent bottles.

Left: Hand molded porcelain teeth dated mid to late 1800s. Vulcanized rubber, called "Vulcanite," was used to fabricate the denture bases. Goodyear owned the Vulcanite patent and any dentist wishing to use the product had to purchase an expensive license to do so.

hygiene (noun)
The preservation of health and prevention of disease.

LOOK GOOD, FEEL GOOD!

Left: Bristled toothbrushes originated in China about 1600 A.D. These bone brushes, minus their hog hair bristles date from the 1800s. Tooth powder often came in porcelain pots.

WOODS ARECA NUT
6d
TOOTH PASTE
For removing Tartar and whitening the Teeth without injuring the Enamel
PROPRIETOR
W. WOODS
CHEMIST
PLYMOUTH

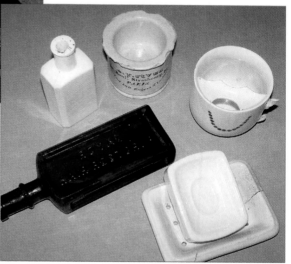

Right: Artifacts of a long ago lifestyle: blue bottle of Royal Hair Restorer; milk glass bottle of Hagan's Magnolia Balm; French cream jar; mustache cup and two soap dishes.

Ask Tom:

What would have been the most often used cosmetic 100 years ago?

GENUINE
YANKEE SOAP,
Manufactured at
MANCHESTER, CONN.,
WILLIAMS & BROTHERS
CHEMISTS AND APOTHECARIES.

Tom Says:

Hair dyes and hair regenerators were popular along with perfumes.

 # Quarts and Pints
= Dairy

cottage cheese (noun)
Soft white cheese made by straining and seasoning the curds of sour milk.

What we know: Most early towns had at least one dairy. Bottles were glass with a "slug plate" molded into the front naming the dairy and town. Empty bottles were returned to be reused.

What we want to know: If bottles were returned to the dairy to be reused, why were so many found in privies?

What we learned: People might change dairies in town or move to another town with a new dairy. Folks knew the dairy only wanted its own bottles returned, thus the unwanted empties were tossed down the privy.

Above: Slug plate for Glen Ellyn, IL dairy.

Above: By the pint or quart, every town had a dairy. A collection of milk bottles from suburban Chicago, IL dairies: West Chicago, Naperville, Wheaton, Glen Ellyn, Aurora.

LIKE I ALWAYS SAY, "IN ONE END, OUT THE UDDER!"

Above: School growth chart emphasizing importance of milk and healthy habits for healthy living.

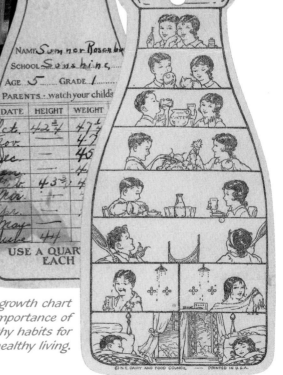

Above: Some suburban Illinois dairies: Towsley of Naperville, Naperville Creamery, Elm Place of Wheaton, Rathbun Farm of Glen Ellyn and Aurora Dairy Co.

Otterpohl

BAKER'S DAIRY PASTEURIZED MILK DOWNERS GROVE ILL.

JOHANSEN DAIRY GENEVA ILL.

Cream Top Milk

1 PT. TODAY

2 QT. TODAY

Compliments of THE STUDIO PRESS Naperville Illinois

HEY! YOU SAP, LEGGO, THAT'S MY NOSE!

Marked: Tichnor Bros. #552. Posted 1947.

Right: Otterpohl Dairy cottage cheese jar from Naperville, IL.

Ask Tom:

Are dairy bottles often found intact? If so, why?

Wishing You Lots of Luck Bud + Betty Bowman

Tom Says:

Ten times more are found broken. Having come into use as privies were going out, milks were found higher in the hole, in the frost line, causing them to crack.

'Round the Table = Fine Dining

china (noun)
A fine porcelain made of clay originally imported from China.

Meals were an occasion in the 1800s. Victorians took pride in setting a fine table and had the dishes and flatware to do it. White ironstone was the most popular and serviceable dishware while blue was the color of choice for decorative china.

Dishes are frequently dug, though most are found broken. Silverware is not often found as metal deteriorates quickly underground. As with many digs, there are often unanswered questions that surface. For instance, why would someone discard a complete set of china, including the soup tureen pictured here, down the privy? Food for thought.

Right: The corrosion on the flatware indicates they are not gold or silver, but common metal.

Left: Salt and pepper shakers are always found as "orphans," never as pairs.

Right: Handleless cups predate those with finger holds. Tea or coffee would be poured from the cup into the saucer to cool for drinking.

Above: Elegant privy survivor.

Above: China platter - a silent puzzle with forever missing pieces.

Right: Variations on the color blue.

Ask Tom:

Can china be used to date a hole?

Toothpick holder.

LOOKS LIKE ALL MY FANCY COUSINS HAVE A CHINA CONNECTION.

Above: Unusually large double-handled sugar bowls. Found without lids.

Tom Says:

No. China could be kept for generations before being discarded and is thus not reliable for dating.

*S*erve It Up = Flasks & Beers

Above: Porcelain beer bottle stoppers.

flask (noun)
A small, flattened container for liquor to be carried in the pocket.

Often plain, sometimes handsome, pocket sized and ready to travel, flasks for whiskey are exciting finds for diggers. Remarkably intact after a century underground, flasks varied in shape from plain and sleek with paper labels to elaborate commemoratives marking major events. Miniatures were given away to mark special occasions. As flasks were not returnable, empties were often pitched down the privy.

Unlike flasks, beer bottles were meant to be returned for refilling, thus fewer are dug. While all early flasks were stopped with corks, some beers featured porcelain stoppers. Though the vessels may be different, the popularity of the brews continues to please palates today.

Above: Two Illinois "blob" beer bottles: Frank Rechenmacher, Naperville; Aurora Brewing Co., Aurora.

Left: Udolpho Wolfe's Aromatic Schnapps bottles.

Below: Two brown beers from New York and Aurora, Illinois.

I FEEL A LITTLE NIP AND IT'S NOT IN THE AIR!

Left: A one-of-a-kind pottery flask and uniquely styled corn ear flask.

Right: Two "pumpkin seed" shaped flasks and one "coffin" shaped flask. All dug in Illinois.

Below: Pretty but plain, five unadorned aqua flasks.

Above: Four patriotic themed flasks: pale green Prussian soldier with German inscription on back that reads, "As long as a soldier can wave a bottle courage will not sink."; aqua "Union" bottle with clasped hands; green George Washington with lyre; aqua double eagle.

Ask Tom:

How do you clean the bottles you dig?

Tom Says:

Dish soap, water and SOS pads can clean outsides. Copper chips and water are shaken to clean insides.

 ᴛake Your Turn = Playthings

Oh, the heartbreak of losing a favorite toy. And down the privy nonetheless! Such was the fate facing many a Victorian child who carted along a cherished marble, toy gun or bubble pipe on a quickie run to the outhouse. One careless move in that darkened interior and - gone forever. Marbles and doll dishes to lie dormant and iron toys to rust and decompose. Until a 21st century history buff probes the site and rescues the fallen treasures, offering us a glimpse of a child's life in the 1800s.

Marked: Rust Craft Shop. Kansas City, MO #844. c1913.

ᴴow many balls can you count here,
ᴀnd which is the largest one
ᴀnd which one is the prettiest
ᴀnd which would you choose for fun?

Above: *A rare find. A Sulphide fish marble. Other Sulphides might depict numbers, people, toys or initials. Smaller than actual size.*

Above: *Two Onionskin marbles, one with a pontil mark, and an Opaque Swirl oiled to bring out its original beauty. Smaller than actual size.*

marble scissors (noun)
Tool used when making marbles that leaves opposing double pontil marks.

Above: *A variety of dug marbles. Note blue and brown glazed clay Benningtons with "eyes" from firing and the Chinese with painted geometric design.*

Above: Children's plates showing raised alphabet border, transfer pattern nursery rhymes and maxims.

Marked: Birthday Series #104. Posted 1914.

Enjoy your little parties
That will make you grow:
I wish you every happiness
Through all your life, you know.

FUN WHILE THEY LASTED.

Below: Child's bank with chiseled opening to retrieve hard earned savings. Actual size.

Above Right: Examples of cast iron toys. Rare finds as iron rusts and usually disintegrates underground.

Right: Finding one or two doll dishes in a hole is not uncommon, but sets are never found. Note the bubble pipe atop the ten inch tall chest and the white souvenir cup on the bottom shelf.

Ask Tom:

What is your most prized marble?

Tom Says:

The Sulfide with the fish inside. That one was dug in Naperville, Illinois.

Under the Bed = Chamber Pots

chamber (noun)

A room in a house, especially a bedroom.

Few welcomed a night trip to the privy, for reasons besides inclement weather. Thus the need for the lidded chamber pot, a.k.a. thunder mug, slop jar, growler or Peggy, just a short reach under the bed. While distasteful to today's sensibilities, it served a need and no bedroom would be without one. But what's used at night needs emptying in the morning. A slip of the hand, a loss of balance and down the hole it went. While common to excavate pots, it is rare to find a lid. Possibly left behind for safe keeping?

Marked: Genuine Curteich - Chicago. "C.T. Art-Colortone."

C-823

BOY! AM I POOPED!

Right, Above Right: Richly decorated inside and out. Manufactured in New York.

Below: Often kept under beds, these plain porcelain pots prevented a nighttime trip to the privy.

Above: An older banded pot.

Left: A lineup of unbroken chamber pots. Two decorative, one banded.

Below: Rare find - pot with lid. Most are found lidless.

Marked: Published by the Asheville Post Card Co.

HAVIN' A FINE TIME HERE, JUST ROUGHING IT AND TAKIN' POT LUCK.

Above: Smaller than chamber pots and with funnel-shaped tops, these spittoons would be openly displayed in Victorian parlors for the convenience of tobacco chewers.

Ask Tom:

Was is unusual for chamber pots to be highly decorative?

HEY! WHAT ARE THESE GUYS DOIN' ON MY PAGE?

Tom Says:

No, it was not unusual for them to be decorative as many were "in sight."

illage Namesake = Naper & Neighbors

Capt. Joseph Naper
Ship's captain who moved from Ohio to establish Naperville in 1831.

Many of Tom's digs have been in Naperville, IL, a suburban community thirty miles west of Chicago. He soon noticed that digs in rural areas were not as rich as those in railroad towns. Because train delivery stocked store shelves with a vast variety of goods, there was less need to repair damaged possessions when newer and better could be easily had.

The arrival of the CB&Q in Naperville in 1864 opened the way to unlimited and ever-changing sources of merchandise. People could buy for reasons other than need and it was all convenient in local stores. Soon, decoration became as important as necessities in every area of living.

Above: Ring dug on site of original Naper home.

Below: Angelic religious figures.

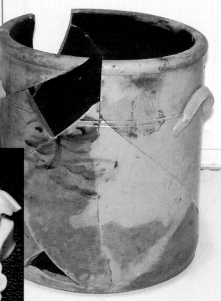

Above: Large crock from privy of Thomas Naper, son of namesake Joseph.

Left: Which came first, the chicken or the egg?

A TOAST TO NAPERVILLE'S 175TH! 1831-2006

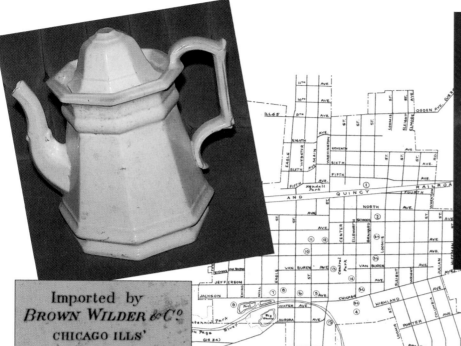

Above: Two high-fashion figurines that would have elevated decorating beyond everyday needs.

Above: Ironstone coffee pot with Chicago maker's mark.

NAPERVILLE

POINTS OF INTEREST

1. Kroehler Mfg. Co. Home Plant
2. Evangelical Theological Seminary
3. North Central College
4. Site of Fort Payne
5. Old New York House
6. Old Egermann Brewery Building
7. Old Stenger Brewery Building
8. Naperville Cheese Co. Building
9. Centennial Park
10. Bethel Church of the Brethren
11. Old Stenger Brewery and Malt House

Ask Tom:

Have you ever decided not to dig even when you had permission?

Undigested fruit and vegetable seeds from bottom of Naper family privy.

Above: Embossed alphabet plate with two Franklin proverbs: "Three removes are as bad as a fire. A rolling stone gathers no moss."

Right: Porcelain pitcher with unusually large lip. Oversize, lidless sugar bowl and patterned dish cover.

Tom Says:

I decided not to dig one site due to a rumor of a relative being buried in the yard.

With Pen in Hand
= Ink Bottles

SANFORD'S BLACK INK

With the spread of literacy in the 1800s, writing became a popular form of expression. The use of first the quill pen and later the steel nib required frequent dipping into ink. Once empty, single use bottles were disposed of - down the privy. Amazingly, many of the glass "inks" survived the fall and cascades of abuse to be unearthed decades later with a light as a whisper coating of "fairy dust," the iridescent frosting of a bygone era.

Above: Aqua glass ink bottles (1865-1915) were most common. Other glass colors were more costly and rare.

pontil (noun)
A glass or iron rod used in glassmaking for handling the hot glass.

It would serve you right Because you don't **WRITE!**

Marked: CS519.

Above and Right: Tall, spouted master ink bottles were used to refill smaller ones.

G.A.H.ZEISS GLORIA-FEDER

April 17th 1836

Below: *Well used blotter absorbed excess ink from nib pens. A necessity on every early desktop.*

Above: *Eight-sided ribbed umbrella style ink bottle. Others had as many as sixteen sides. Glass bottles need tender care if dug in cold weather. They must be wrapped to avoid shattering from sudden exposure to freezing temperatures when lifted from the hole where dirt temperatures average in the fifties.*

A drop of Ink makes Millions think.

Bulwer Lytton

Paid
Rev Orange Lyman
Downers Grove
Dupage Co
Illinois

Do you do RIGHT when you don't WRITE?

Marked: c1909 by H.H. Tammen, Denver.

Above: *Ink bottle with open pontil scar created by a glass rod used to lift the form from its mold.*

Little drops of ink
Little grains of wit
Make for lazy letter writers
Postal cards to fit

HOW TO WRITE LETTERS   CROWTHER   GARDEN CITY PUBLISHING CO.

Left: *Note variety of ink bottle shapes.*

OH, FOR A BALL POINT PEN!

GLASS — AVOID FREEZING.
Stafford's
THE INK THAT ABSORBS
MOISTURE FROM THE AIR
NEW YORK—CHICAGO. U.S.A

Above: Although expensive, ink was available in a variety of colors. Not privy dug.

MEYER &
WENTHE
CHICAGO

REICHE HARDWARE
VAR CO.

REICHE & COMPANY
NAPERVILLE, ILL.

MABIE
TODD
& C·o
NEW·YORK
G

Left: Hand stamps from a Naperville, Illinois business. Not privy dug.

Ask Tom:

Why do the aqua bottles look iridescent?

Above: A collection of pottery ink bottles (1870-1900). Good for travel, they were sturdy and did not tip easily. Cone-shaped examples were called "cone inks."

Tom Says:

The acidity of the soil etches the glass and causes the iridescence. I call it 'fairy dust.'

e**X**ceptionally Weird = UFOs

Above: Strange bedfellows. A perfume atomizer inside a carved conch shell.

> **verdigris** (noun)
> A green coating that forms like rust on brass, bronze or copper.

Test your skill on these Unidentified "Found" Objects, but don't look for an answer key because there isn't one. It's not as easy as it looks. There's always a twist. How and where the items were used are key questions. Unsolved mysteries from privy digs, they are not from out of this world, just from out of our time.

Above: Can you find the boy, book and dog on this metal UFO?

Right: Two music related hollow sleeves? Marked on rims: 4M. 3042 Quartette. Characteristic Negro Medly. Pat'd July 29, '02; 4M. 3020 Sketch. The Arkansas Traveler. Spencer. Pat'd July 29, '02.

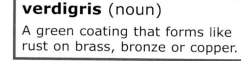

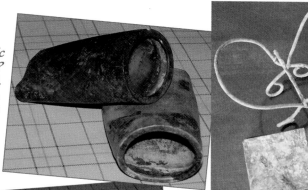

Above: Mysteries in metal: object with holes; hinged case; oversized wall bracket; V-shaped holder; heavy, inscribed, ID link band.

Left: Small ceramic questions with no certain answers. First glance suggests the blue piece is a bud vase, but the tiny opening would defy the slenderest of stems.

Ask Tom:

Have you ever been stumped by a UFO you were later able to identify?

Above: Smoke bell.

Tom Says:

Yes. A smoke bell. It was an item suspended over a kerosene lamp to prevent black soot from accumulating on the ceiling.

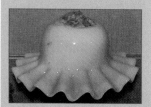

YOUR GUESS IS AS GOOD AS MINE.

 **oung at Heart** = Dolls

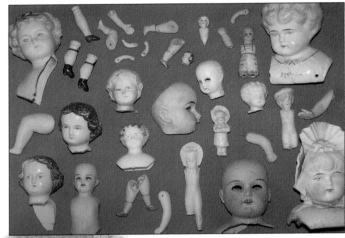

limb (noun)
An arm or a leg.

Almost every little girl falls in love early - with a favorite doll. Sadly, outhouse holes are full of their ghosts. Digs commonly yield china heads, arms and mostly legs, but rarely in pairs. Ninety percent are badly broken, probably discarded as unsuitable playmates. Debuted around 1840, china heads and limbs were sewn to stuffed cloth bodies and hearts melted - and broke, either from a shattering drop or an unthinkable plunge "down the hole."

Below: An assortment of unearthed doll parts. Blonde head (1904), top right, shows hole where cloth body was attached. Note also her decorative gold collar and name, Bertha.

British card marked: A&H "Cheer-O" series, #287.

Broke as you are, I love you.

FRED SPURGIN

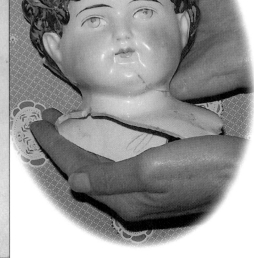

Left: Black hair most common color. Curly style dates head from mid to late 1800s.

Above: Diminutive darlings, many with hats.

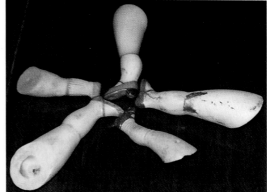

Above: High kickers from the Victorian Age.

Right: Hairstyles on these three beauties rank them by stage of life. A child's short boy's bob, a young lady's curled bob and a matron's center part with buns arranged on each side.

Above: One-piece dolls were called Frozen Charlottes or Frozen Charlies. Made in Germany, starting in the 1850s, they rarely cost more than a quarter.

Left: Four varied examples of excavated dolls. Blonde hair, introduced around 1870, was less common than black hair.

HEADS AND HEARTS ARE EASILY BROKEN.

Marked: Made in U.S.A. CS439. Posted 1913.

Above: Doll size potty and decorative feature for child's chamber pot.

Postcard unmarked.

Doll and Drum Party

at_____ on next _____ afternoon, from_____ until_____ o'clock

Each girl must bring her dolly
Each boy his horn or drum
Our party will be jolly
Tell mama she must come

> LOOK! EVEN DOLLY HAD HER OWN POTTY!

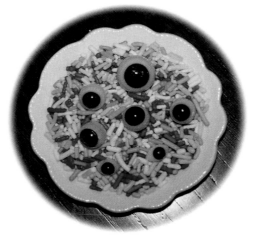

Above: Frozen Charlottes boast their own Victorian cautionary legend. A winter storm, an open air ride, a spurned warm coat and, alas, a frozen, headstrong child at journey's end.

Ask Tom:

Seeing all these limbs raises the question, have you ever found any real bones?

Above: A dish of doll eyes. Some mechanical called "sleep eyes" and some bisque that would have been glued in.

Right: Kewpie doll. Actual size.

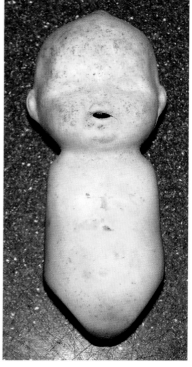

Tom Says:

No human bones. All animal bones. Mostly kitchen scraps.

Zany = Styles & Monikers

While most privies were simple wooden affairs, some were quite unique in name and style. But whatever the name, the purpose was the same.

321

NO MATTER WHERE WE ROAM, IT'S JUST HOME SWEET HOME!

FIDO · SITTING ROOM · PARLOR

Marked: "Tichnor Quality Views." Boston, MA.

I'M ON THE ANXIOUS SEAT — WAITING TO HEAR FROM YOU

BUSY

Marked: Colourpicture Publication. Boston, MA.

847

Marked: Stanley A. Piltz Co., San Francisco, CA.

REST ROOM

FULNER FOTO · "END OF..."

6A-H2860

Marked: F.J. McCollom 1963. Far West Studios.
Virginia City, Montana.

Whatever the name . . .

Dooley
Back House
Pokey
Biffy
Willie
Closet
Throne Room
Reading Room
Necessary
Nessy

Chapel of Ease
Comfort Station
Sears Booth
Eleanor
Chick Sales
Uncle John
Aunt Sue
Trip to the Woodpile
Trip to the Rose Bush

NOW THAT YOU'VE READ THE BOOK AND SEEN THE PICTURES, DO YOU DIG IT?!

Tom Says:

An unbroken egg, two shotguns and brass knuckles.

Ask Tom:

What are some favorite objects you have dug thus far?

THE END

Sources

Bader, Dr. Myles H. *20,001 Food Facts, Chefs Secrets & Household Hints.* Bader Publishing, LLC, 2004 ed.

Fletcher, Nick. *The A-Z of 100 Popular Collectables.* London: Word Lock Ltd., 1986.

Grist, Everett. *Antique and Collectible Marbles, 3rd ed.* Paducah, KY: Collector Books, 1992.

Kovel, Terry H. and Ralph M. *Dictionary of Marks - Pottery and Porcelain.* New York: Crown Publishers, 1971.

McClinton, Katharine Morrison. *Antiques of American Childhood.* New York: Bramhall House, 1970.

Ode to the Outhouse: A Tribute to a Vanishing American Icon. Stillwater, MN: Voyageur Press, 2002.

Moving on to new digs.